Tunisian Shawls

LEISURE ARTS, INC. • Maumelle, Arkansas

EDITORIAL STAFF
Vice President of Editorial: Susan White Sullivan
Creative Art Director: Katherine Laughlin
Publications Director: Leah Lampirez
Special Projects Director: Susan Frantz Wiles
Technical Writer: Lois J. Long
Technical Editors: Linda A. Daley, Sarah J. Green,
   and Cathy Hardy
Art Category Manager: Lora Puls
Graphic Artist: Cailen Cochran
Prepress Technician: Stephanie Johnson
Contributing Photographer: Ken West
Contributing Photo Stylist: Sondra Daniel

BUSINESS STAFF
President and Chief Executive Officer:
   Fred F. Pruss
Senior Vice President of Operations:
   Jim Dittrich
Vice President of Retail Sales:
   Martha Adams
Controller: Tiffany P. Childers
Information Technology Director: Brian Roden
Director of E-Commerce: Mark Hawkins
Manager of E-Commerce: Robert Young

ISBN-13/EAN: 978-1-4647-1657-7

Meet the Designer

A lifelong crafter, Sharon Hernes Silverman says
Tunisian crochet is her true passion. "I like to
experiment with different stitch patterns because
of the unique fabric that results," she says. "I love
to learn new things. This openness to innovation
keeps my work interesting for me and for the
people who use my patterns." Because shawls come
in a variety of shapes and styles, they provide the
perfect opportunity for crocheters to master Tunisian
techniques and to create beautiful projects, she says.
Other books of Sharon's designs include Tunisian
Crochet Baby Blankets, available in stores nationwide
and on LeisureArts.com. Sharon also maintains an
active presence on Ravelry and Facebook and has a
blog at SharonSilverman.com.

A former travel writer, writing instructor, and
restaurant reviewer, she is based in West Chester,
Pennsylvania. She and her husband have two
college-age sons.

9

13

5

17

19

23

31

27

Get the look of knitting with the ease of crochet in these 8 gorgeous wraps featuring yarns from fine to bulky. They'll take you through all the seasons!

Expanding Vees

Worked from the top down, this two-color triangle gets its drama from increasingly wide stripes in two different stitch patterns. Fine-weight yarn gives the wrap excellent drape and makes it surprisingly lightweight for its size.

 **EASY +**

Finished Size: 49½" wide x 28" deep (125.5 cm x 71 cm)

SHOPPING LIST

Yarn (Fine Weight) **FINE 2**

[3.5 ounces, 307 yards
(100 grams, 281 meters) per skein]:

☐ Black - 2 skeins

☐ Cream - 1 skein

Tunisian Hook

Minimum length 22" (56 cm)

☐ Size K (6.5 mm)

   or size needed for gauge

Standard Crochet Hook

☐ Size J (6 mm)

Additional Supplies

☐ Split-ring marker

GAUGE INFORMATION

With Tunisian hook,

16 tss and 13 rows = 4" (10 cm)

Please refer to gauge on page 41.

STITCH GUIDE

📷 Tunisian Simple Stitch *(Fig. 3, page 43)*

📷 Tunisian Knit Stitch *(Fig. 4, page 43)*

📷 Make One *(Fig. 10, page 45)*

INSTRUCTIONS

With Tunisian hook and Cream, ch 7.

Foundation Row (Right side): 📷 Pull up a loop in horizontal bar of second ch from hook and each ch across, close *(Figs.1a-c, page 43)*: 7 tss.

The stitch count on each row increases by 4 stitches. The increases are made after the first vertical bar, on each side of the middle stitch, and before the last stitch. A marker is placed on the middle stitch of each row, moving it from row to row as you work.

Row 1: Skip first vertical bar, M1, work 2 tks, M1, work tks, place marker around loop just made, M1, work 2 tks, M1, work tks, close: 11 sts.

Rows 2-16: Skip first vertical bar, M1, work tks across to marked st, M1, remove marker, work tks, place marker around loop just made, M1, work tks across to last st, M1, work tks, close: 71 sts.

Row 17: Skip first vertical bar, M1, work tks across to marked st, M1, remove marker, work tks, place marker around loop just made, M1, work tks across to last st, M1, work tks, close changing to Black in last st *(Fig. 13, page 46)*; cut Cream: 75 sts.

Rows 18-22: Skip first vertical bar, M1, work tss across to marked st, M1, remove marker, work tss, place marker around loop just made, M1, work tss across to last st, M1, work tss, close: 95 sts.

Row 23: Skip first vertical bar, M1, work tss across to marked st, M1, remove marker, work tss, place marker around loop just made, M1, work tss across to last st, M1, work tss, close changing to Cream in last st; cut Black: 99 sts.

Rows 24 and 25: Skip first vertical bar, M1, work tks across to marked st, M1, remove marker, work tks, place marker around loop just made, M1, work tks across to last st, M1, work tks, close: 107 sts.

Row 26: Skip first vertical bar, M1, work tks across to marked st, M1, remove marker, work tks, place marker around loop just made, M1, work tks across to last st, M1, work tks, close changing to Black in last st; cut Cream: 111 sts.

Rows 27-34: Skip first vertical bar, M1, work tss across to marked st, M1, remove marker, work tss, place marker around loop just made, M1, work tss across to last st, M1, work tss, close: 143 sts.

Row 35: Skip first vertical bar, M1, work tss across to marked st, M1, remove marker, work tss, place marker around loop just made, M1, work tss across to last st, M1, work tss, close changing to Cream in last st; cut Black: 147 sts.

Rows 36 and 37: Skip first vertical bar, M1, work tks across to marked st, M1, remove marker, work tks, place marker around loop just made, M1, work tks across to last st, M1, work tks, close: 155 sts.

Row 38: Skip first vertical bar, M1, work tks across to marked st, M1, remove marker, work tks, place marker around loop just made, M1, work tks across to last st, M1, work tks, close changing to Black in last st; cut Cream: 159 sts.

Rows 39-49: Skip first vertical bar, M1, work tss across to marked st, M1, remove marker, work tss, place marker around loop just made, M1, work tss across to last st, M1, work tss, close: 203 sts.

Row 50: Skip first vertical bar, M1, work tss across to marked st, M1, remove marker, work tss, place marker around loop just made, M1, work tss across to last st, M1, work tss, close changing to Cream in last st; cut Black: 207 sts.

Rows 51 and 52: Skip first vertical bar, M1, work tks across to marked st, M1, remove marker, work tks, place marker around loop just made, M1, work tks across to last st, M1, work tks, close: 215 sts.

Row 53: Skip first vertical bar, M1, work tks across to marked st, M1, remove marker, work tks, place marker around loop just made, M1, work tks across to last st, M1, work tks, close changing to Black in last st; cut Cream: 219 sts.

Rows 54-67: Skip first vertical bar, M1, work tss across to marked st, M1, remove marker, work tss, place marker around loop just made, M1, work tss across to last st, M1, work tss, close: 275 sts.

Instructions continued on page 15.

Cables & Heart

There's a little present embraced by the "hugs and kisses" cables in this season-spanning shawl: a textured heart at the center back. Don't worry if the cables work up a bit ruffly: a good blocking relaxes them into place.

 **INTERMEDIATE**

Finished Size: 46½" wide x 18" high (118 cm x 45.5 cm)

SHOPPING LIST

Yarn (Light Weight)
[3.5 ounces, 306 yards
(100 grams, 280 meters) per skein]:
☐ 4 skeins

Tunisian Hook
Minimum length 22" (56 cm)
☐ Size K (6.5 mm)
   or size needed for gauge

Standard Crochet Hook
☐ Size H (5 mm)

Additional Supplies
☐ Cable needle

GAUGE INFORMATION

With Tunisian hook, 19 tps and 16 rows = 4" (10 cm)

one repeat = 3¾" (9.5 cm)

Please refer to gauge on page 41.

STITCH GUIDE

Tunisian Simple Stitch *(Fig. 3, page 43)*

Tunisian Knit Stitch *(Fig. 4, page 43)*

Tunisian Purl Stitch *(Fig. 5, page 44)*

Tunisian Reverse Stitch *(Fig. 6, page 44)*

Back Cable (uses next 6 sts)

Work 3 tks **loosely**, slip 3 tks just made onto a cable needle and hold at **back** *(Fig. A)*, work 3 tks **loosely**, slip 3 tks from cable needle onto hook *(Fig. B)*.

Fig. A

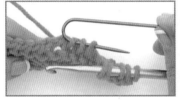

Fig. B

Front Cable (uses next 6 sts)

Work 3 tks **loosely**, slip 3 tks just made onto a cable needle and hold at **front** *(Fig. C)*, work 3 tks **loosely**, slip 3 tks from cable needle onto hook *(Fig. D)*.

Fig. C

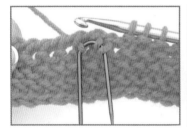

Fig. D

INSTRUCTIONS

With Tunisian crochet hook, ch 224.

Foundation Row (Right side): With yarn in front of work, pull up a loop in second ch from hook as for tps *(Fig. E)* and in each ch across, close: 224 tps.

Fig. E

Rows 1 and 2: Skip first vertical bar, work tps across to last st, work tss, close.

When working the closing across the Cables, pull the loops apart as you work, being careful to draw through 2 loops at a time, not 3.

Row 3: Skip first vertical bar, work 6 tps, work (Back Cable, Front Cable, 6 tps) across to last st, work tss, close: 24 Cables.

Rows 4-6: Skip first vertical bar, work 6 tps, work (12 tks, 6 tps) across to last st, work tss, close.

Row 7: Skip first vertical bar, work 6 tps, work (Front Cable, Back Cable, 6 tps) across to last st, work tss, close.

Rows 8-10: Skip first vertical bar, work 6 tps, work (12 tks, 6 tps) across to last st, work tss, close.

Rows 11-18: Repeat Rows 3-6 twice.

Rows 19-22: Repeat Rows 7-10.

Row 23: Skip first vertical bar, work (6 tps, Front Cable, Back Cable) 5 times, work 42 tps, work (Front Cable, Back Cable, 6 tps) across to last st, work tss, close.

Rows 24-26: Skip first vertical bar, work (6 tps, 12 tks) 5 times, work 3 tps, work 36 tks, work 3 tps, work (12 tks, 6 tps) across to last st, work tss, close.

Row 27: Skip first vertical bar, work (6 tps, Back Cable, Front Cable) 5 times, work 3 tps, work 18 tks, work trs, work 17 tks, work 3 tps, work (Back Cable, Front Cable, 6 tps) across to last st, work tss, close.

Row 28: Skip first vertical bar, work (6 tps, 12 tks) 5 times, work 3 tps, work 17 tks, work 3 trs, work 16 tks, work 3 tps, work (12 tks, 6 tps) across to last st, work tss, close.

Row 29: Skip first vertical bar, work (6 tps, 12 tks) 5 times, work 3 tps, work 16 tks, work 5 trs, work 15 tks, work 3 tps, work (12 tks, 6 tps) across to last st, work tss, close.

Row 30: Skip first vertical bar, work (6 tps, 12 tks) 5 times, work 3 tps, work 15 tks, work 7 trs, work 14 tks, work 3 tps, work (12 tks, 6 tps) across to last st, work tss, close.

Row 31: Skip first vertical bar, work (6 tps, Back Cable, Front Cable) 5 times, work 3 tps, work 14 tks, work 9 trs, work 13 tks, work 3 tps, work (Back Cable, Front Cable, 6 tps) across to last st, work tss, close.

Row 32: Skip first vertical bar, work (6 tps, 12 tks) 5 times, work 3 tps, work 13 tks, work 11 trs, work 12 tks, work 3 tps, work (12 tks, 6 tps) across to last st, work tss, close.

Row 33: Skip first vertical bar, work (6 tps, 12 tks) 5 times, work 3 tps, work 12 tks, work 13 trs, work 11 tks, work 3 tps, work (12 tks, 6 tps) across to last st, work tss, close.

Row 34: Skip first vertical bar, work (6 tps, 12 tks) 5 times, work 3 tps, work 11 tks, work 15 trs, work 10 tks, work 3 tps, work (12 tks, 6 tps) across to last st, work tss, close.

Row 35: Skip first vertical bar, work (6 tps, Front Cable, Back Cable) 5 times, work 3 tps, work 10 tks, work 17 trs, work 9 tks, work 3 tps, work (Front Cable, Back Cable, 6 tps) across to last st, work tss, close.

Rows 36 and 37: Skip first vertical bar, work (6 tps, 12 tks) 5 times, work 3 tps, work 10 tks, work 17 trs, work 9 tks, work 3 tps, work (12 tks, 6 tps) across to last st, work tss, close.

Row 38: Skip first vertical bar, work (6 tps, 12 tks) 5 times, work 3 tps, work 10 tks, work 8 trs, work tks, work 8 trs, work 9 tks, work 3 tps, work (12 tks, 6 tps) across to last st, work tss, close.

Row 39: Skip first vertical bar, work (6 tps, Front Cable, Back Cable) 5 times, work 3 tps, work 10 tks, work 7 trs, work 3 tks, work 7 trs, work 9 tks, work 3 tps, work (Front Cable, Back Cable, 6 tps) across to last st, work tss, close.

Row 40: Skip first vertical bar, work (6 tps, 12 tks) 5 times, work 3 tps, work 11 tks, work 5 trs, work 5 tks, work 5 trs, work 10 tks, work 3 tps, work (12 tks, 6 tps) across to last st, work tss, close.

Row 41: Skip first vertical bar, work (6 tps, 12 tks) 5 times, work 3 tps, work 12 tks, work 3 trs, work 7 tks, work 3 trs, work 11 tks, work 3 tps, work (12 tks, 6 tps) across to last st, work tss, close.

Row 42: Skip first vertical bar, work (6 tps, 12 tks) 5 times, work 3 tps, work 36 tks, work 3 tps, work (12 tps, 6 tks) across to last st, work tss, close.

Instructions continued on page 15.

Autumn Embrace

Rich with blended autumn hues, this quick and easy shawl is sure to become your go-to wrap for fall activities. Reach for it as you head out for pumpkin-picking, football games, or to view the changing leaves.

 **EASY**

Finished Size: 50" wide x 17" high (127 cm x 43 cm), excluding fringe

SHOPPING LIST

Yarn (Bulky Weight) **BULKY 5**

[3 ounces, 90 yards
(85 grams, 81 meters) per skein]:

☐ 6 skeins

Tunisian Hook

Minimum length 22" (56 cm)

☐ Size N/P (10 mm)

or size needed for gauge

Standard Crochet Hook

☐ Size L (8 mm)

GAUGE INFORMATION

With Tunisian hook,

10 tds = 4" (10 cm); 4 rows = 4½" (11.5 cm);

10 tfs and 12 rows = 4" (10 cm)

Please refer to gauge on page 41.

━━━ STITCH GUIDE ━━━

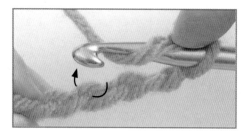 Tunisian Simple Stitch *(Fig. 3, page 43)*

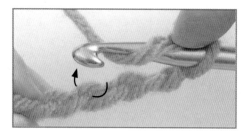 Tunisian Full Stitch *(Fig. 7, page 44)*

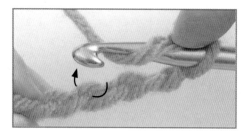 Tunisian Double Stitch *(Figs. 8a & b, page 44)*

INSTRUCTIONS

With Tunisian crochet hook, ch 124, place marker in fifth ch from hook to mark st placement.

Foundation Row (Right side): YO, insert hook in third ch from hook *(Fig. A)*, YO and pull a loop, YO and draw through 2 loops on hook **(tds made)**, work tds in next ch and in each ch across, close: 123 tds.

Fig. A

Rows 1-3: Ch 1, skip first vertical bar, work tds across, close.

Row 4: Skip first 2 vertical bars, work tfs across to last st, work tss, close: 121 tfs and 2 tss.

Row 5: Skip first vertical bar, work tfs across to last 2 vertical bars, skip next vertical bar, work tss, close: 121 tfs and 2 tss.

Rows 6-23: Repeat Rows 4 and 5, 6 times; then repeat Row 4 once **more**: 121 tfs and 2 tss.

Rows 24-26: Ch 1, skip first vertical bar, work tds across, close.

Row 27 (Bind off row)**:** With standard crochet hook, ch 1, skip first vertical bar, ★ YO, insert hook in next vertical bar as for tss, YO and pull up a loop, (YO and draw through 2 loops on hook) twice **(dc made)**; repeat from ★ across; do **not** finish off.

See Crochet Stitches, page 46.

TRIM

Ch 1, sc evenly across end of rows, ch 15, slip st in second ch from hook and in each ch across **(fringe made)**; working in free loops of beginning ch *(Fig. 2, page 42)*, sc in first 5 chs, ch 15, slip st in second ch from hook and in each ch across **(fringe made)**, ★ sc in next 6 chs, ch 15, slip st in second ch from hook and in each ch across **(fringe made)**; repeat from ★ across to marked ch, remove marker, sc in next 4 chs, ch 15, slip st in second ch from hook and in each ch across **(fringe made)**, sc evenly across end of rows; working across last row, sc in each dc across; join with slip st to first sc, finish off.

EXPANDING VEES

Continued from page 7.

Row 68: Skip first vertical bar, M1, work tss across to marked st, M1, remove marker, work tss, place marker around loop just made, M1, work tss across to last st, M1, work tss, close changing to Cream in last st; cut Black: 279 sts.

Row 69: Skip first vertical bar, M1, work tks across to marked st, M1, remove marker, work tks, place marker around loop just made, M1, work tks across to last st, M1, work tks, close: 283 sts.

Row 70: Skip first vertical bar, M1, work tks across to marked st, M1, remove marker, work tks, place marker around loop just made, M1, work tks across to last st, M1, work tks, close; do **not** cut Cream: 287 sts.

See Crochet Stitches, page 46.

TRIM

Rnd 1: With standard crochet hook, skip first vertical bar, insert hook in next sp, YO and pull up a loop, YO and draw through both loops on hook **(sc made)**, sc as for tks in each st across to marked st, remove marker, sc in next sp, sc in next st, place marker around sc just made, sc in next sp, sc as for tks in each st across to last st, 3 sc as for tks in last st; sc evenly across end of rows; 3 sc in corner; join with slip st to first sc, finish off.

Rnd 2: With **wrong** facing, join Black with sc in same st as joining; sc in each sc across to center sc of next 3-sc group, 3 sc in center sc, sc in each sc across to marked sc, 3 sc in marked sc, remove marker, sc in each sc across to center sc of next 3-sc group, 3 sc in center sc, sc in last sc; join to first sc with slip st, finish off.

CABLES AND HEART

Continued from page 11.

Row 43: Skip first vertical bar, work (6 tps, Back Cable, Front Cable) 5 times, work 42 tps, work (Back Cable, Front Cable, 6 tps) across to last st, work tks, close.

Rows 44-46: Skip first vertical bar, work 6 tps, work (12 tks, 6 tps) across to last st, work tss, close.

Rows 47-50: Repeat Rows 43-46.

Rows 51-58: Repeat Rows 7-10 twice.

Row 59: Skip first vertical bar, work 6 tps, work (Back Cable, Front Cable, 6 tps) across to last st, work tss, close: 24 cables.

Rows 60 and 61: Skip first vertical bar, work tps across to last st, work tss, close.

Row 62 (Bind off row)**:** With standard crochet hook, skip first vertical bar, ★ inserting hook as for tps, YO and pull a loop, YO and draw through both loops on hook **(sc made)**; repeat from ★ across; finish off.

Block Shawl *(see Blocking, page 47)*.

Hot Pink Lace

Cotton bamboo yarn is an excellent choice
for warm-weather shawls. Ribbing borders
openwork in this cheerful rectangle.

 **EASY**

Finished Size: 11" wide x 57½" high (28 cm x 146 cm)

SHOPPING LIST

Yarn (Light Weight) **③ LIGHT**
[3.5 ounces, 245 yards
(100 grams, 224 meters) per skein]:
☐ 3 skeins

Tunisian Hook

Minimum length 22" (56 cm)
☐ Size K (6.5 mm)
or size needed for gauge

Standard Crochet Hook

☐ Size I (5.5 mm)

Instructions continued on page 21.

Silver Shimmer

The wing-like shape of this shiny shawl adds elegance for a dressy occasion. For everyday wear, choose a more casual yarn.

 **INTERMEDIATE**

Finished Size: 54" wide at widest point x 7½" high (137 cm x 19 cm)

SHOPPING LIST

Yarn (Medium Weight)

[3 ounces, 252 yards
(85 grams, 230 meters) per skein]:

☐ 2 skeins

Tunisian Hook

Minimum length 22" (56 cm)

☐ Size K (6.5 mm)

or size needed for gauge

Standard Crochet Hook

☐ Size I (5.5 mm)

GAUGE INFORMATION

With Tunisian hook, one repeat = 4½" (11.5 cm);
   12 rows = 6" (15.25 cm)

Please refer to gauge on page 41.

STITCH GUIDE

Tunisian Simple Stitch *(Fig. 3, page 43)*
Tunisian Double Stitch *(Figs. 8a & b, page 44)*

INSTRUCTIONS

With Tunisian hook, ch 228.

Foundation Row (Right side): Pull up a loop in horizontal bar of second ch from hook and each ch across, close *(Figs. 1a-c, page 43)*: 228 tss.

Row 1: Skip first vertical bar, work tss across, close.

Row 2: Ch 2, work 4 tds in first vertical bar, work tds, (skip next st, work tds) 8 times, ★ work 5 tds in each of next 2 sts, work tds, (skip next st, work tds) 8 times; repeat from ★ across to last st, work 5 tds in last st, close.

Row 3: Skip first vertical bar, work tss across, close.

Row 4: Skip first vertical bar, slip st in next 19 sts *(Fig. 14, page 46)*, ch 2, work 4 tds in same st as last slip st, work tds, (skip next st, work tds) 8 times, ★ work 5 tds in each of next 2 sts, work tds, (skip next st, work tds) 8 times; repeat from ★ 8 times **more**, work 5 tds in next st, leave remaining sts unworked, close: 190 tds.

Row 5: Skip first vertical bar, work tss across, close.

Row 6: Skip first vertical bar, slip st in next 19 sts, ch 2, work 4 tds in same st as last slip st, work tds, (skip next st, work tds) 8 times, ★ work 5 tds in each of next 2 sts, work tds, (skip next st, work tds) 8 times; repeat from ★ 6 times **more**, work 5 tds in next st, leave remaining sts unworked, close: 152 tds.

Row 7: Skip first vertical bar, work tss across, close.

Row 8: Skip first vertical bar, slip st in next 19 sts, ch 2, work 4 tds in same st as last slip st, work tds, (skip next st, work tds) 8 times, ★ work 5 tds in each of next 2 sts, work tds, (skip next st, work tds) 8 times; repeat from ★ 4 times **more**, work 5 tds in next st, leave remaining sts unworked, close: 114 tds.

Row 9: Skip first vertical bar, work tss across, close.

Row 10: Skip first vertical bar, slip st in next 19 sts, ch 2, work 4 tds in same st as last slip st, work tds, (skip next st, work tds) 8 times, ★ work 5 tds in each of next 2 sts, work tds, (skip next st, work tds) 8 times; repeat from ★ 2 times **more**, work 5 tds in next st, leave remaining sts unworked, close: 76 tds.

Row 11: Skip first vertical bar, work tss across, close.

Row 12: Skip first vertical bar, slip st in next 19 sts, ch 2, work 4 tds in same st as last slip st, work tds, (skip next st, work tds) 8 times, work 5 tds in each of next 2 sts, work tds, (skip next st, work tds) 8 times, work 5 tds in next st, leave remaining sts unworked, close: 38 tds.

Row 13: Skip first vertical bar, work tss across, close.

Row 14: With standard crochet hook, skip first vertical bar, ★ slip st as for tss in each st across; work slip st in end of next 2 rows; repeat from ★ 5 times **more**; finish off.

HOT PINK LACE
Continued from page 17.

GAUGE INFORMATION

With Tunisian hook, in Rib Pattern,

   12 sts = 3" (7.5 cm); 6 rows = 2" (5 cm)

   Body Pattern, 14 sts = 3½" (9 cm); 4 rows = 4" (10 cm)

Please refer to gauge on page 41.

──── STITCH GUIDE ────

Tunisian Simple Stitch *(Fig. 3, page 43)*

Tunisian Knit Stitch *(Fig. 4, page 43)*

Tunisian Purl Stitch *(Fig. 5, page 44)*

INSTRUCTIONS
BOTTOM RIB PATTERN

With Tunisian crochet hook, ch 231.

Foundation Row (Right side): With yarn in front of work, pull up a loop in second ch from hook as for tps *(Fig. E, page 10)* and in next ch, pull up a loop in next 3 chs as for tss, (pull up a loop in next 3 chs as for tps, pull up a loop in next 3 chs as for tss) across to last 3 chs, pull up a loop in next 2 chs as for tps, pull up a loop in last ch as for tss, close: 115 tps and 116 tss.

Rows 1-5: Skip first vertical bar, work 2 tps, work 3 tks, work (3 tps, 3 tks) across to last 3 sts, work 2 tps, work tss, close: 115 tps, 114 tks, and 2 tss.

BODY

Row 1: Skip first vertical bar, work tks across to last st, work tss, close: 229 tks and 2 tss.

Row 2: Skip first vertical bar, ★ insert hook under next 2 vertical bars at same time, YO and pull up loop, YO *(Fig. A)*; repeat from ★ across to last 2 sts, work 2 tss, close.

Fig. A

Row 3: Skip first vertical bar, ★ work tss, insert hook from **front** to **back** in next sp, YO and pull up loop; repeat from ★ across to last 2 sts, work 2 tss, close.

Rows 4-27: Repeat Rows 2 and 3, 12 times.

Row 28: Skip first vertical bar, work tks across to last st, work tss, close.

TOP RIB PATTERN

Rows 1-5: Skip first vertical bar, work 2 tps, work 3 tks, work (3 tps, 3 tks) across to last 2 sts, work 2 tps, work tss, close.

See Crochet Stitches, page 46.

Row 6 (Bind off row): With standard crochet hook, skip first vertical bar, insert hook in next st as for tks, YO and pull up a loop, YO and through both loops on hook **(sc made)**, sc as for tks in next st and in each st across to last st, 3 sc as for tks in last st; sc in end of each row across; working in free loops of beginning ch *(Fig. 2, page 42)*, 3 sc in first ch, sc in next ch and in each ch across to last ch, 3 sc in last ch; sc in end of each row across, 3 sc in first st of last row; join with slip st to first sc, finish off.

Popover Wedges

Short-row wedges nestle together with offset points for a fun-loving look. Multicolor yarn provides an exciting blend of colors.

■■■□ **INTERMEDIATE**

Finished Size: 12" (30.5 cm) across neckline, 24½" (62 cm) across widest point, 12½" (32 cm) from neck to bottom point of wedges

SHOPPING LIST

Yarn (Medium Weight)
[3.5 ounces, 151 yards
(100 grams, 138 meters) per skein]:
☐ 3 skeins

Tunisian Hook
Minimum length 22" (56 cm)
☐ Size K (6.5 mm)
    or size needed for gauge

Standard Crochet Hooks
☐ Size H (5 mm) **and**
☐   Size K (6.5 mm)

Additional Supplies
☐ Yarn needle

GAUGE INFORMATION

With Tunisian hook, 15 tss and 12 rows = 4" (10 cm)

STITCH GUIDE

📹 Tunisian Simple Stitch (*Fig. 3, page 43*)
📹 Chain Cast On (*Figs. 12a-d, page 46*)

INSTRUCTIONS
FIRST WEDGE

With Tunisian hook, ch 60.

Foundation Row (Right side): 📹 Pull up a loop in horizontal bar of second ch from hook and each ch across, close (*Figs. 1a-c, page 43*): 60 tss.

With each row, 3 additional stitches are left unworked.

Rows 1-19: Skip first vertical bar, work tss across to last 3 sts, leave remaining 3 sts unworked, close: 3 tss.

Each wedge is offset from the previous wedge. The first row of a new wedge is 12 sts less at the beginning and is 12 sts more at the end.

SECOND THRU EIGHTH WEDGE

Row 1: Skip first vertical bar, slip st in next 2 vertical bars as for tss (*Fig. 14, page 46*), working in unworked tss on previous rows, slip st in next 10 tss as for tss, the loop on the hook is the first st, work 47 tss, with larger size standard crochet hook, chain cast on 12 loops, close: 60 tss.

For the final 12 sts on each repeat of Row 2, you will be working into the Chain Cast On sts. The vertical bars may look a little shorter than standard vertical bars. Stretch those stitches with your fingers to identify them.

Row 2: Skip first vertical bar, work tss across to last 3 sts, leave remaining 3 sts unworked, close: 57 tss.

With each row, 3 additional stitches are left unworked.

Rows 3-20: Skip first vertical bar, work tss across to last 3 tss, leave remaining 3 tss unworked: 3 tss.

Bind Off Row: With smaller size standard crochet hook, skip first vertical bar, slip st in next 2 vertical bars, working in unworked tss on previous rows, slip st in each tss as for tss across to point of wedge, finish off.

FINISHING

With **wrong** side facing, align first and last wedges with a 12-stitch offset to keep wedges in pattern. Sew edges together.

📹 *See Crochet Stitches, page 46.*

NECK BAND

Rnd 1: With **right** side facing and using smaller size standard crochet hook, join yarn with slip st at seam on neck edge; ch 3 (**counts as first dc**), work 103 dc evenly spaced around; join with slip st to first dc: 104 dc.

📹 To work sc2tog, pull up a loop in each of next 2 dc, YO and draw through all 3 loops on hook (**counts as one sc**).

Rnd 2: Ch 1, turn; sc in first 4 dc, (sc2tog, sc in next 3 dc) around; join with slip st to first sc, finish off.

Red Hot Wrap

Spice up your wardrobe with this vivid red shawl! Tunisian openwork stitches create airy stripes through the dense Tunisian honeycomb fabric. A giant tassel finishes off each end of the flowing oblong shape.

■■■◻ **INTERMEDIATE**

Finished Size: 67" wide x 20" high (170 cm x 51 cm)

SHOPPING LIST

Yarn (Light Weight) **3** LIGHT

[3.5 ounces, 340 yards
(100 grams, 310 meters) per skein]:

☐ 4 skeins

Tunisian Hook

Minimum length 22" (56 cm)

☐ Size K (6.5 mm)

or size needed for gauge

Standard Crochet Hook

☐ Size I (5.5 mm)

Additional Supplies

☐ Tapestry needle

GAUGE INFORMATION

With Tunisian hook, in pattern,
   17 sts and 13 rows = 4" (10 cm)
Please refer to gauge on page 41.

STITCH GUIDE

Tunisian Simple Stitch *(Fig. 3, page 43)*
Tunisian Purl Stitch *(Fig. 5, page 44)*
Tunisian Double Stitch *(Figs. 8a & b, page 44)*

INSTRUCTIONS

With Tunisian hook, ch 284.

Foundation Row (Right side): With yarn in front of work, pull up a loop in second ch from hook as for tps *(Fig. E, page 10)*, ★ pull up a loop in next ch as for tss, pull up a loop in next ch as for tps; repeat from ★ across to last 2 chs, pull up a loop in last 2 chs as for tss, close: 284 sts.

Row 1: Skip first vertical bar, work tss, work (tps, tss) across, close.

Row 2: Skip first vertical bar, work tps, work (tss, tps) across to last 2 sts, work 2 tss, close.

Row 3: Skip first vertical bar, work tss, work (tps, tss) across, close.

Row 4:
Step A (Forward Pass) - Ch 2 **(counts as first tds)**, ★ skip next 2 sts, work tds in next st, work tds in first skipped st; repeat from ★ across to last st, work tds: 190 loops.

Step B (Return Pass) - YO and draw through one loop on hook, YO and draw through 2 loops on hook, ★ ch 1, (YO and draw through 2 loops) twice; repeat from ★ across: 190 sts and 94 ch-1 sps.

Row 5: Skip first vertical bar, work tss, ★ insert hook from **front** to **back** in next ch-1 sp, YO and pull up a loop, work 2 tss; repeat from ★ across, close: 284 sts.

Row 6: Skip first vertical bar, work tps, work (tss, tps) across to last 2 sts, work 2 tss, close.

Row 7: Skip first vertical bar, work tss, work (tps, tss) across.

Rows 8 and 9: Repeat Rows 6 and 7.

Rows 10-49: Repeat Rows 4-9, 6 times; then repeat Rows 4-7 once **more**.

Row 50 (Bind off row): With standard crochet hook, skip first vertical bar, insert hook as for tps, YO and pull up a loop, YO and draw through both loops on hook **(sc made)**, ★ sc in next st as for tss, sc in next st as for tps; repeat from ★ across to last 2 sts, sc in last 2 sts as for tss; finish off.

GATHERING

Thread tapestry needle with a piece of yarn approximately 50" (127 cm) long. With **right** side facing and beginning at center of one short edge, weave needle through ends of rows from the center to the outer edge, then back to the center. Weave needle through ends of rows to the opposite outer edge, then back to the center. Gently pull ends until the edge is gathered. Tie ends in a knot.

Repeat across opposite short end.

TASSEL (Make 2)

Cut a piece of cardboard 3" wide x 8" long (7.5 cm x 20.5 cm). Wind a double strand of yarn around the cardboard approximately 30 times. Cut an 18" (45.5 cm) length of yarn and insert it under all of the strands at the top of the cardboard; pull up **tightly** and tie securely. Leave the yarn ends long enough to attach the tassel. Cut the yarn at the opposite end of the cardboard *(Fig. A)* and then remove it. Cut a 16" (40.5 cm) length of yarn and wrap it **tightly** around the tassel twice, 1" (2.5 cm) below the top *(Fig. B)*; tie securely. Trim the ends.

Attach one Tassel to center of each end of Shawl.

Fig. A

Fig. B

Fair Isle Winter Capelet

Stranded colorwork puts the geometric design front and center on this delightfully warm capelet. Using two colors in any given row, the working color is pulled up in the right spot to match the pattern, with the unused color carried across the back. Follow the chart and you'll get the hang of this interesting technique in no time.

 **INTERMEDIATE**

SHOPPING LIST

Yarn (Medium Weight) **4**
[3.5 ounces, 165 yards
(100 grams, 150 meters) per skein]:
- ☐ Cream - 2 skeins
- ☐ Dk Blue - 1 skein
- ☐ Blue - 1 skein
- ☐ Grey - 1 skein

Tunisian Hook

Minimum length 22" (56 cm)
- ☐ Size K (6.5 mm)

    or size needed for gauge

Standard Crochet Hook

- ☐ Size I (5.5 mm)

Additional Supplies

- ☐ Yarn needle

SIZE INFORMATION

Circumference at lower edge:

40{44-48½}"/101.5{112-123} cm

Length:

14{15-16¼}"/35.5{38-41.5} cm

Size Note: We have printed the instructions for the sizes in different colors to make it easier for you to find:

• Small/Medium in Blue

• Large in Pink

• X-Large in Green

Instructions in Black apply to all sizes.

GAUGE INFORMATION

With Tunisian hook, 18 tss and

13 rows = 4" (10 cm)

───── **STITCH GUIDE** ─────

🎥 Tunisian Simple Stitch *(Fig. 3, page 43)*

🎥 Tss2tog *(Figs. 11a & b, page 45)*

PRACTICE SWATCH

Work the Practice Swatch to get comfortable with changing colors and stranding the yarn.

Finished Size: 4½" x 2¼" (11.5 cm x 5.75 cm)

The pattern is a multiple of 10 sts.

With Cream and using Tunisian hook, ch 20.

Foundation Row (Right side): 🎥 Pull up a loop in horizontal bar of second ch from hook and each ch across, close *(Figs. 1a-c, page 43)*: 20 tss.

Row 1: Skip first vertical bar, work tss across, close
🎥 changing to Dk Blue in last st *(Fig. 13, page 46)*.

Work same as Rows 1-5 of Pattern Band **or** follow Chart A, page 40, for 5 rows.

Cut Cream and finish off Dk Blue.

INSTRUCTIONS
BOTTOM BORDER

With Tunisian hook and using Cream, ch 180{200-220}.

Foundation Row (Right side): 🎥 With yarn in front of work as for tps, pull up a loop in second ch from hook *(Fig. E, page 10)* and in each ch across, close: 180{200-220} sts.

Size Small/Medium ONLY

Row 1: Skip first vertical bar, work tss across, close
🎥 changing Dk Blue in last st *(Fig. 13, page 46)*.

Size Large ONLY

Rows 1 and 2: Skip first vertical bar, work tss across, close.

Row 3: Skip first vertical bar, work tss across, close
🎥 changing Dk Blue in last st *(Fig. 13, page 46)*.

Size X-Large ONLY

Rows 1-4: Skip first vertical bar, work tss across, close.

Row 5: Skip first vertical bar, work tss across, close
🎥 changing Dk Blue in last st *(Fig. 13, page 46)*.

CHANGING COLORS

Do **not** cut yarn unless instructed. 🎥 Carry unused yarn loosely across **wrong** side *(Fig. A)*. When closing, 🎥 change to next color when one loop of the previous color remains on the hook *(Fig. B)*.

When the first stitch on the next row is a different color than the last stitch on the closing, complete the last stitch with the first color of the next row.

Fig. A

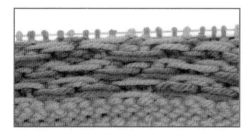

Fig. B

PATTERN BAND

If desired, you can follow Chart Instructions on page 40 following Chart A.

Row 1:
Step A (Forward Pass) - Skip first vertical bar, with Dk Blue, work tss, drop Dk Blue, with Cream, work 3 tss, ★ with Dk Blue, work 2 tss, with Cream, work 3 tss; repeat from ★ across.
Step B (Return Pass) - With Cream, (YO and draw through one loop on hook, YO and draw through 2 loops on hook) twice, drop Cream, with Dk Blue, (YO and draw through 2 loops on hook) twice, ★ (with Cream, YO and draw through 2 loops on hook) 3 times, (with Dk Blue, YO and draw through 2 loops on hook) twice: repeat from ★ across.

Continue to change colors in same manner.

Row 2: Skip first vertical bar, with Dk Blue, work tss, with Cream, work 2 tss, with Dk Blue, work tss, with Cream, work 2 tss, with Dk Blue, work tss, with Cream, work 2 tss, ★ with Dk Blue, work 2 tss, with Cream, work 2 tss, with Dk Blue, work tss, with Cream, work 2 tss, with Dk Blue, work tss, with Cream, work 2 tss; repeat from ★ across, close changing to Cream in last st.

Row 3: Skip first vertical bar, with Cream, work 2 tss, with Dk Blue, work tss, ★ with Cream, work 4 tss, with Dk Blue, work tss; repeat from ★ across to last st, with Cream, work tss, close.

Row 4: Skip first vertical bar, with Cream, work tss, with Dk Blue, work tss, with Cream, work 2 tss, with Dk Blue, work 2 tss, with Cream, work 2 tss, with Dk Blue, work tss, ★ with Cream, work 2 tss, with Dk Blue, work tss, with Cream, work 2 tss, with Dk Blue, work 2 tss, with Cream, work 2 tss, with Dk Blue, work tss; repeat from ★ across, close changing to Dk Blue in last st.

Row 5: Skip first vertical bar, with Dk Blue, work tss, with Cream, work 3 tss, ★ with Dk Blue, work 2 tss, with Cream, work 3 tss; repeat from ★ across, close changing to Cream in last st; cut Dk Blue.

SOLID BAND

You will use 2 strands of Cream, using one strand at a time, changing strands every 3 stitches on the forward pass and the return pass. The stranding of the Cream will keep the weight of the Solid Bands the same as the Pattern Bands.

Size Small/Medium ONLY

Row 1: Skip first vertical bar, work tss across, close.

Row 2: Skip first vertical bar, work tss across, close changing to Blue in last st; cut one strand of Cream.

Rows 1-3: Skip first vertical bar, work tss across, close.

Row 4: Skip first vertical bar, work tss across, close changing to Blue in last st; cut one strand of Cream.

Size X-Large ONLY

Rows 1-5: Skip first vertical bar, work tss across, close.

Row 6: Skip first vertical bar, work tss across, close changing to Blue in last st; cut one strand of Cream.

BODY PATTERN

If desired, you can follow Chart Instructions on page 40 following Chart B.

Row 1: Skip first vertical bar, (with Cream, work tss, with Blue, work tss) 3 times, with Cream, work 2 tss, with Blue, work 3 tss, with Cream, work 2 tss, ★ with Blue, work tss, (with Cream, work tss, with Blue, work tss) 6 times, with Cream, work 2 tss, with Blue, work 3 tss, with Cream, work 2 tss; repeat from ★ across to last 6 tss, (with Blue, work tss, with Cream, work tss) 3 times, close changing to Cream in last st.

Row 2: Skip first vertical bar, with Blue, work tss, (with Cream, work tss, with Blue, work tss) twice, with Cream, work 4 tss, with Blue, work tss, with Cream, work 4 tss, ★ with Blue, work tss, (with Cream, work tss, with Blue, work tss) 5 times, with Cream, work 4 tss, with Blue, work tss, with Cream, work 4 tss; repeat from ★ across to last 5 tss, with Blue, work tss, (with Cream, work tss, with Blue, work tss) twice, close changing to Blue in last st.

Row 3: Skip first vertical bar, (with Cream, work tss, with Blue, work tss) twice, with Cream, work 4 tss, with Blue, work 3 tss, with Cream, work 4 tss, ★ with Blue, work tss, (with Cream, work tss, with Blue, work tss) 4 times, with Cream, work 4 tss, with Blue, work 3 tss, with Cream, work 4 tss; repeat from ★ across to last 4 tss, (with Blue, work tss, with Cream, work tss) twice, close changing to Cream in last st.

Row 4: Skip first vertical bar, with Blue, work tss, with Cream, work tss, with Blue, work tss, with Cream, work 4 tss, with Blue, work 2 tss, with Cream, work tss, with Blue, work 2 tss, with Cream, work 4 tss, ★ with Blue, work tss, (with Cream, work tss, with Blue, work tss) 3 times, with Cream, work 4 tss, with Blue, work 2 tss, with Cream, work tss, with Blue, work 2 tss, with Cream, work 4 tss; repeat from ★ across to last 3 tss, with Blue, work tss, with Cream, work tss, with Blue, work tss, close changing to Blue in last st.

Row 5: Skip first vertical bar, with Cream, work tss, with Blue, work tss, with Cream, work 3 tss, (with Blue, work 3 tss, with Cream, work 3 tss) twice, ★ with Blue, work tss, (with Cream, work tss, with Blue, work tss) twice, with Cream, work 3 tss, (with Blue, work 3 tss, with Cream, work 3 tss) twice; repeat from ★ across to last 2 tss, with Blue, work tss, with Cream, work tss, close changing to Cream in last st.

Row 6: Skip first vertical bar, with Blue, work tss, with Cream, work 2 tss, with Blue, work 3 tss, with Cream, work 3 tss, with Blue, work tss, with Cream, work 3 tss, with Blue, work 3 tss, with Cream, work 2 tss, with Blue, work tss, ★ with Cream, work tss, with Blue, work tss, with Cream, work 2 tss, with Blue, work 3 tss, with Cream, work 3 tss, with Blue, work tss, with Cream, work 3 tss, with Blue, work 3 tss, with Cream, work 2 tss, with Blue, work tss; repeat from ★ across, close changing to Blue in last st.

Row 7: Skip first vertical bar, (with Cream, work 2 tss, with Blue, work 2 tss) twice, with Cream, work tss, with Blue, work tss, with Cream, work tss, (with Blue, work 2 tss, with Cream, work 2 tss) twice, ★ with Blue, work tss, (with Cream, work 2 tss, with Blue, work 2 tss) twice, with Cream, work tss, with Blue, work tss, with Cream, work tss, (with Blue, work 2 tss, with Cream, work 2 tss) twice; repeat from ★ across, close changing to Grey in last st; cut Cream.

Row 8: Skip first vertical bar, with Grey, work tss, (with Blue, work 2 tss, with Grey, work 2 tss) twice, with Blue, work tss, (with Grey, work 2 tss, with Blue, work 2 tss) twice, with Grey, work 3 tss, ★ (with Blue, work 2 tss, with Grey, work 2 tss) twice, with Blue, work tss, (with Grey, work tss, with Blue, work 2 tss) twice; repeat from ★ across to last tss, with Grey, work tss, close.

Row 9: Skip first vertical bar, with Blue, work 2 tss, with Grey, work 2 tss, with Blue, work tss, with Grey, work tss, with Blue, work 2 tss, with Grey, work tss, with Blue, work tss, with Grey, work tss, with Blue, work 2 tss, with Grey, work tss, with Blue, work tss, with Grey, work 2 tss, with Blue, work 2 tss, ★ with Grey, work tss, with Blue, work 2 tss, with Grey, work 2 tss, with Blue, work tss, with Grey, work tss, with Blue, work 2 tss, with Grey, work tss, with Blue, work tss, with Grey, work tss, with Blue, work 2 tss, with Grey, work tss, with Blue, work tss, with Grey, work 2 tss, with Blue, work 2 tss; repeat from ★ across, close.

Row 10: Skip first vertical bar, with Blue, work 2 tss, with Grey, work 5 tss, with Blue, work tss, (with Grey, work tss, with Blue, work tss) twice, with Grey, work 5 tss, with Blue, work 2 tss, ★ with Grey, work tss, with Blue, work 2 tss, with Grey, work 5 tss, with Blue, work tss, (with Grey, work tss, with Blue, work tss) twice, with Grey, work 5 tss, with Blue, work 2 tss; repeat from ★ across, close.

Row 11: Skip first vertical bar, with Blue, work 2 tss, with Grey, work tss, with Blue, work 2 tss, with Grey, work 2 tss, with Blue, work tss, with Grey, work 3 tss, with Blue, work tss, with Grey, work 2 tss, with Blue, work 2 tss, ★ (with Grey, work tss, with Blue, work 2 tss) 3 times, with Grey, work 2 tss, with Blue, work tss, with Grey, work 3 tss, with Blue, work tss, with Grey, work 2 tss, with Blue, work 2 tss; repeat from ★ across to last 3 tss, with Grey, work tss, with Blue, work 2 tss, close.

Row 12: Skip first vertical bar, with Blue, work 2 tss, with Grey, work tss, with Blue, work tss, with Grey, work 2 tss, with Blue, work 2 tss, with Grey, work tss, with Blue, work tss, with Grey, work tss, with Blue, work 2 tss, with Grey, work 2 tss, with Blue, work tss, with Grey, work tss, ★ (with Blue, work 2 tss, with Grey, work tss) twice, with Blue, work tss, with Grey, work 2 tss, with Blue, work 2 tss, with Grey, work tss, with Blue, work tss, with Grey, work tss, with Blue, work 2 tss, with Grey, work 2 tss, with Blue, work tss, with Grey, work tss; repeat from ★ across to last 2 tss, with Blue, work 2 tss, close.

Row 13: Skip first vertical bar, with Blue, work 2 tss, with Grey, work tss, with Blue, work tss, with Grey, work tss, (with Blue, work 3 tss, with Grey, work tss, with Blue, work tss, with Grey, work tss) twice, with Blue, work 2 tss, ★ with Grey,
work tss, with Blue, work 2 tss, with Grey, work tss, with Blue, work tss, with Grey, work tss, (with Blue, work 3 tss, with
Grey, work tss, with Blue, work tss, with Grey, work tss) twice, with Blue, work 2 tss; repeat from ★ across, close.

Row 14: Skip first vertical bar, with Blue, work 2 tss, with Grey, work tss, with Blue, work 4 tss, with Grey, work tss, (with Blue, work tss, with Grey, work tss) twice, with Blue, work 4 tss, with Grey, work tss, ★ (with Blue, work 2 tss, with Grey, work tss) twice, with Blue, work 4 tss, with Grey, work tss, (with Blue, work tss, with Grey, work tss) twice, with Blue, work 4 tss, with Grey, work tss; repeat from ★ across to last 2 sts, with Blue, work 2 tss, close.

Row 15: Skip first vertical bar, with Blue, work 3 tss, with Grey, work tss, with Blue, work tss, (with Grey, work 4 tss, with Blue, work tss) twice, ★ (with Grey, work tss, with Blue, work 3 tss) twice, with Grey, work tss, with Blue, work tss, (with Grey, work 4 tss, with Blue, work tss) twice; repeat from ★ across to last 4 sts, with Grey, work tss, with Blue, work 3 tss, close.

Row 16: Skip first vertical bar, with Grey, work tss, with Blue, work 2 tss, with Grey, work 3 tss, with Blue, work tss, with Grey, work tss, with Blue, work 3 tss, with Grey, work tss, with Blue, work tss, with Grey, work 3 tss, with Blue, work 2 tss, ★ with Grey, work 3 tss, with Blue, work 2 tss, with Grey, work 3 tss, with Blue, work tss, with Grey, work tss, with Blue, work 3 tss, with Grey, work tss, with Blue, work tss, with Grey, work 3 tss, with Blue, work 2 tss; repeat from ★ across to last tss, with Grey, work tss, close changing to Dk Blue in last st; cut Blue.

Row 17: Skip first vertical bar, with Grey, work tss, (with Dk Blue, work 3 tss, with Grey, work 2 tss, with Dk Blue, work 3 tss, with Grey, work tss) twice, ★ with Dk Blue, work tss, with Grey, work tss, (with Dk Blue, work 3 tss, with Grey, work 2 tss, with Dk Blue, work 3 tss, with Grey, work tss) twice; repeat from ★ across, close.

Row 18: Skip first vertical bar, with Dk Blue, work tss, with Grey, work tss, with Dk Blue, work 2 tss, with Grey, work 2 tss, with Dk Blue, work 2 tss, with Grey, work tss, with Dk Blue, work tss, with Grey, work tss, with Dk Blue, work 2 tss, with Grey, work 2 tss, with Dk Blue, work 2 tss, with Grey, work tss, ★ with Dk Blue, work 3 tss, with Grey, work tss, with Dk Blue, work 2 tss, with Grey, work 2 tss, with Dk Blue, work 2 tss, with Grey, work tss, with Dk Blue, work 2 tss, with Grey, work tss, with Dk Blue, work 2 tss, with Grey, work 2 tss, with Dk Blue, work 2 tss, with Grey, work tss; repeat from ★ across to last tss, with Dk Blue, work tss, close.

Row 19: Skip first vertical bar, with Grey, work 3 tss, with Dk Blue, work 2 tss, with Grey, work 2 tss, with Dk Blue, work 2 tss, with Grey, work tss, with Dk Blue, work 2 tss, with Grey, work 2 tss, with Dk Blue, work 2 tss, with Grey, work 3 tss, ★ with Dk Blue, work tss, with Grey, work 3 tss, with Dk Blue, work 2 tss, with Grey, work 2 tss, with Dk Blue, work 2 tss, with Grey, work tss, with Dk Blue, work 2 tss, with Grey, work 2 tss, with Dk Blue, work 2 tss, with Grey, work 3 tss; repeat from ★ across, close.

Row 20: Skip first vertical bar, with Grey, work 4 tss, with Dk Blue, work 3 tss, (with Grey, work tss, with Dk Blue, work 3 tss) twice, with Grey, work 4 tss, ★ with Dk Blue, work tss, with Grey, work 4 tss, with Dk Blue, work 3 tss, (with Grey, work tss, with Dk Blue, work 3 tss) twice, with Grey, work 4 tss; repeat from ★ across, close.

Row 21: Skip first vertical bar, with Grey, work tss, with Dk Blue, work tss, with Grey, work 3 tss, with Dk Blue, work 3 tss, with Grey, work tss, with Dk Blue, work tss, with Grey, work tss, with Dk Blue, work 3 tss, with Grey, work 3 tss, with Dk Blue, work tss, ★ (with Grey, work tss, with Dk Blue, work tss) twice, with Grey, work 3 tss, with Dk Blue, work 3 tss, with Grey, work tss, with Dk Blue, work tss, with Grey, work tss, with Dk Blue, work 3 tss, with Grey, work 3 tss, with Dk Blue, work tss; repeat from ★ across to last tss, with Grey, work tss, close changing to Cream in last st; cut Grey.

Row 22: Skip first vertical bar, with Dk Blue, work tss, with Cream, work 3 tss, with Dk Blue, work tss, with Cream, work 2 tss, with Dk Blue, work 5 tss, with Cream, work 2 tss, with Dk Blue, work tss, with Cream, work 3 tss, with Dk Blue, work tss, ★ with Cream, work tss, with Dk Blue, work tss, with Cream, work 3 tss, with Dk Blue, work tss, with Cream, work 2 tss, with Dk Blue, work 5 tss, with Cream, work 2 tss, with Dk Blue, work tss, with Cream, work 3 tss, with Dk Blue, work tss; repeat from ★ across, close changing to Dk Blue in last st.

Row 23: Skip first vertical bar, with Cream, work tss, with Dk Blue, work 5 tss, with Cream, work 2 tss, with Dk Blue, work 3 tss, with Cream, work 2 tss, with Dk Blue, work 5 tss, with Cream, work tss, ★ with Dk Blue, work tss, with Cream, work tss, with Dk Blue, work 5 tss, with Cream, work 2 tss, with Dk Blue, work 3 tss, with Cream, work 2 tss, with Dk Blue, work 5 tss, with Cream, work tss; repeat from ★ across, close changing to Cream in last st.

Row 24: Skip first vertical bar, with Dk Blue, work tss, with Cream, work 3 tss, with Dk Blue, work tss, (with Cream, work 4 tss, with Dk Blue, work tss) twice, with Cream, work 3 tss, with Dk Blue, work tss, ★ with Cream, work tss, with Dk Blue, work tss, with Cream, work 3 tss, with Dk Blue, work tss, (with Cream, work 4 tss, with Dk Blue, work tss) twice, with Cream, work 3 tss, with Dk Blue, work tss; repeat from ★ across, close changing to Dk Blue in last st.

Row 25: Skip first vertical bar, with Cream, work tss, with Dk Blue, work tss, with Cream, work 2 tss, with Dk Blue, work tss, with Cream, work 3 tss, with Dk Blue, work 3 tss, with Cream, work 3 tss, with Dk Blue, work tss, with Cream, work 2 tss, with Dk Blue, work tss, ★ (with Cream, work tss, with Dk Blue, work tss) twice, with Cream, work 2 tss, with Dk Blue, work tss, with Cream, work 3 tss, with Dk Blue, work 3 tss, with Cream, work 3 tss, with Dk Blue, work tss, with Cream, work 2 tss, with Dk Blue, work tss; repeat from ★ across to last tss, with Cream, work tss, close.

Row 26: Skip first vertical bar, with Cream, work 2 tss, with Dk Blue, work tss, with Cream, work 4 tss, with Dk Blue, work 2 tss, with Cream, work tss, with Dk Blue, work 2 tss, with Cream, work 4 tss, with Dk Blue, work tss, ★ (with Cream, work 2 tss, with Dk Blue, work tss) twice, with Cream, work 4 tss, with Dk Blue, work 2 tss, with Cream, work tss, with Dk Blue, work 2 tss, with Cream, work 4 tss, with Dk Blue, work tss; repeat from ★ across to last 2 tss, with Cream, work 2 tss, close.

Row 27: Skip first vertical bar, with Cream, work 3 tss, with Dk Blue, work tss, with Cream, work 3 tss, with Dk Blue, work 2 tss, with Cream, work tss, with Dk Blue, work 2 tss, with Cream, work 3 tss, ★ (with Dk Blue, work tss, with Cream, work 3 tss) 3 times, with Dk Blue, work 2 tss, with Cream, work tss, with Dk Blue, work 2 tss, with Cream, work 3 tss; repeat from ★ across to last 4 tss, with Dk Blue, work tss, with Cream, work 3 tss, close.

Row 28: Skip first vertical bar, with Dk Blue, work tss, with Cream, work 3 tss, with Dk Blue, work tss, with Cream, work 3 tss, ★ with Dk Blue, work 3 tss, with Cream, work 3 tss, with Dk Blue, work tss, with Cream, work 3 tss; repeat from ★ across to last tss, with Dk Blue, work tss, close.

Row 29: Skip first vertical bar, with Cream, work 3 tss, with Dk Blue, work tss, with Cream, work tss, with Dk Blue, work tss, ★ (with Cream, work 3 tss, with Dk Blue, work tss) twice, with Cream, work tss, with Dk Blue, work tss; repeat from ★ across to last 3 tss, with Cream, work 3 tss, close changing to Cream in last st; cut Dk Blue.

SHOULDER SHAPING

You will use 2 strands of Cream for Row 1, using one strand at a time, changing strands every 3 stitches on the forward pass and the return pass.

Row 1: Skip first vertical bar, work tss across, close; cut one strand of Cream.

Row 2: Skip first vertical bar, work 6 tss, work tss2tog, ★ work 9 tss, work tss2tog; repeat from ★ across to last 6{4-2} tss, work 6{4-2} tss, close changing to Blue in last st: 164{182-200} tss.

Row 3: Skip first vertical bar, work 3 tss, work tss2tog, ★ work 4 tss, work tss2tog; repeat from ★ across to last 2 tss, work 2 tss, close: 137{152-167} tss.

Row 4: Skip first vertical bar, work 3 tss, work tss2tog, ★ work 4 tss, work tss2tog; repeat from ★ across to last 5{2-5} tss, work 5{2-5} tss, close changing to Grey in last st: 115{127-140} tss.

Row 5: Skip first vertical bar, work 3 tss, work tss2tog, ★ work 4 tss, work tss2tog; repeat from ★ across to last 1{1-2} tss, work 1{1-2} tss, close: 96{106-117} tss.

Row 6: Skip first vertical bar, work tss across, close.

Row 7 (Bind off row)**:** With standard crochet hook, skip first vertical bar, ★ insert hook under next vertical bar, pull up a loop, YO and draw through 2 loops on hook (**sc made**); repeat from ★ across; finish off.

Sew end of rows together, matching pattern to form back seam.

CHART INSTRUCTIONS

FOLLOWING A CHART

The unworked vertical bar on the right edge of each row is the first stitch on the chart.

Each row is worked in two parts - forward pass and close (return pass).

Follow stitch repeat across each row.

CHANGING COLORS

Do **not** cut yarn unless instructed. 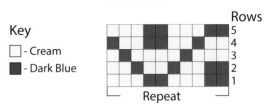 Carry unused yarn loosely across **wrong** side *(Fig. A, page 33)*. When closing, change to next color when one loop of the previous color remains on the hook *(Fig. B, page 33)*.

When the first stitch on the next row is a different color than the last stitch on the closing, complete the last stitch with the first color of the next row.

PATTERN BAND

Rows 1-5: Follow Chart A; cut Dk Blue.

SOLID BAND

Work Solid Band, page 35.

BODY PATTERN

Rows 1-29: Follow Chart B Rows 1-29; cut Dk Blue.

SHOULDER SHAPING

Work Shoulder Shaping, page 39.

CHART A

Key
☐ - Cream
■ - Dark Blue

CHART B

Key
☐ - Cream
■ - Blue
■ - Grey
■ - Dark Blue

General Instructions

ABBREVIATIONS

ch(s)	chain(s)
cm	centimeters
dc	double crochet(s)
M1	Make One
mm	millimeters
Rnd(s)	Round(s)
sc	single crochet(s)
sc2tog	single crochet 2 together
sp(s)	space(s)
st(s)	stitch(es)
tds	Tunisian Double Stitch
tfs	Tunisian Full Stitch
tks	Tunisian Knit Stitch
tps	Tunisian Purl Stitch
trs	Tunisian Reverse Stitch
tss	Tunisian Simple Stitch
tss2tog	Tunisian Simple Stitch 2 together
YO	yarn over

SYMBOLS & TERMS

★ — work instructions following ★ as many **more** times as indicated in addition to the first time.

( ) or **[ ]** — work enclosed instructions **as many** times as specified by the number immediately following **or** contains explanatory remarks.

colon (:) — the number(s) given after a colon at the end of a row denote(s) the number of stitches you should have on that row.

GAUGE

Exact gauge is **essential** for proper size. Before beginning your project, make a sample swatch in the yarn and hook specified in the individual instructions. After completing the swatch, measure it, counting your stitches and rows carefully. If your swatch is larger/smaller than specified **make another, changing hook size to get the correct gauge.** Keep trying until you find the size hook that will give you the specified gauge.

CROCHET TERMINOLOGY

UNITED STATES		INTERNATIONAL
slip stitch (slip st)	=	single crochet (sc)
single crochet (sc)	=	double crochet (dc)
half double crochet (hdc)	=	half treble crochet (htr)
double crochet (dc)	=	treble crochet(tr)
treble crochet (tr)	=	double treble crochet (dtr)
double treble crochet (dtr)	=	triple treble crochet (ttr)
triple treble crochet (tr tr)	=	quadruple treble crochet (qtr)
skip	=	miss

Yarn Weight Symbol & Names	LACE 0	SUPER FINE 1	FINE 2	LIGHT 3	MEDIUM 4	BULKY 5	SUPER BULKY 6
Type of Yarns in Category	Fingering, 10-count crochet thread	Sock, Fingering Baby	Sport, Baby	DK, Light Worsted	Worsted, Afghan, Aran	Chunky, Craft, Rug	Bulky, Roving
Crochet Gauge* Ranges in Single Crochet to 4" (10 cm)	32-42 double crochets**	21-32 sts	16-20 sts	12-17 sts	11-14 sts	8-11 sts	5-9 sts
Advised Hook Size Range	Steel*** 6,7,8 Regular hook B-1	B-1 to E-4	E-4 to 7	7 to I-9	I-9 to K-10.5	K-10.5 to M-13	M-13 and larger

*GUIDELINES ONLY: The chart above reflects the most commonly used gauges and hook sizes for specific yarn categories.

** Lace weight yarns are usually crocheted on larger-size hooks to create lacy openwork patterns. Accordingly, a gauge range is difficult to determine. Always follow the gauge stated in your pattern.

*** Steel crochet hooks are sized differently from regular hooks—the higher the number the smaller the hook, which is the reverse of regular hook sizing.

CROCHET HOOKS

U.S.	B-1	C-2	D-3	E-4	F-5	G-6	7	H-8	I-9	J-10	K-10½	L-11	M/N-13	N/P-15	P/Q	Q	S
Metric - mm	2.25	2.75	3.25	3.5	3.75	4	4.5	5	5.5	6	6.5	8	9	10	15	16	19

■□□□ **BEGINNER**	Projects for first-time crocheters using basic stitches. Minimal shaping.
■■□□ **EASY**	Projects using yarn with basic stitches, repetitive stitch patterns, simple color changes, and simple shaping and finishing.
■■■□ **INTERMEDIATE**	Projects using a variety of techniques, such as basic lace patterns or color patterns, mid-level shaping and finishing.
■■■■ **EXPERIENCED**	Projects with intricate stitch patterns, techniques and dimension, such as non-repeating patterns, multi-color techniques, fine threads, small hooks, detailed shaping and refined finishing.

FOUNDATION ROW

Chain the number indicated in the pattern.

Forward Pass: Pull up a loop in horizontal bar of second ch from hook and each ch across *(Fig. 1a)*.

To Close (Return Pass)**:** YO and draw through one loop on hook **(ch 1 made)** *(Fig. 1b)*, (YO and draw through 2 loops on hook) across *(Fig. 1c)*: one loop.

Fig. 1a

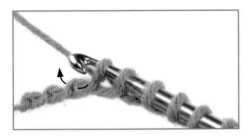

Fig. 1b

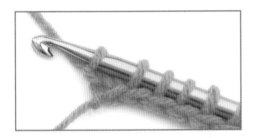

Fig. 1c

FREE LOOPS OF BEGINNING CHAIN

Work into loop(s) indicated *(Fig. 2)*.

Fig. 2

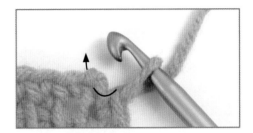

TUNISIAN SIMPLE STITCH
(abbreviated tss)

Insert hook from **right** to **left** under next vertical bar *(Fig. 3)*, YO and pull up a loop.

Fig. 3

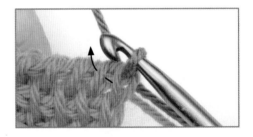

TUNISIAN KNIT STITCH *(abbreviated tks)*

Insert hook from **front** to **back** between front and back vertical bars of next st *(Fig. 4)*, YO and pull up a loop.

Fig. 4

TUNISIAN PURL STITCH *(abbreviated tps)*

With yarn in **front** of work, insert hook from **right** to **left** under next vertical bar, YO and pull up a loop *(Fig. 5)*.

Fig. 5

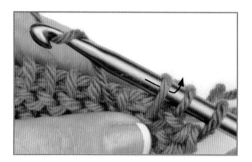

TUNISIAN FULL STITCH *(abbreviated tfs)*

Insert hook from **front** to **back** under horizontal bar between two sts *(Fig. 7)*, YO and pull up a loop.

Fig. 7

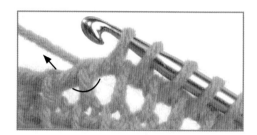

TUNISIAN REVERSE STITCH *(abbreviated trs)*

With yarn in **back** of work, insert hook from **right** to **left** under next **back** vertical bar *(Fig. 6)*, YO and pull up a loop.

Fig. 6

TUNISIAN DOUBLE STITCH *(abbreviated tds)*

YO, insert hook from **front** to **back** between front and back vertical bars of next stitch, YO and pull up a loop, YO and draw through 2 loops on hook *(Figs. 8a & b)*.

Fig. 8a

Fig. 8b

TUNISIAN CROSSED STITCH (uses 2 sts)

Skip next vertical bar, insert hook from **right** to **left** under next vertical bar *(Fig. 9a)*, YO and pull up a loop, insert hook from **right** to **left** under skipped vertical bar, YO and pull up a loop *(Fig. 9b)*.

Fig. 9a

Fig. 9b

MAKE ONE *(abbreviated M1)*

Insert hook from **front** to **back** under horizontal bar between two sts *(Fig. 10)*, YO and pull up a loop.

Fig. 10

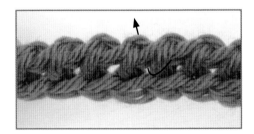

TUNISIAN SIMPLE STITCH 2 TOGETHER *(abbreviated tss2tog)*

Insert hook from **right** to **left** under next 2 vertical bars, YO and draw through 2 loops on hook *(Figs. 11a & b)*.

Fig. 11a

Fig. 11b

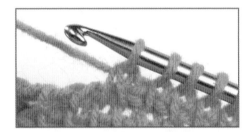

CHAIN CAST ON

Once the forward pass of a row is completed, turn the work so the **wrong** side is facing you.

Insert standard crochet hook under the front vertical bar of the last stitch made, YO and pull up a loop *(Fig. 12a)*.

Fig. 12a

To ch 1 around the Tunisian hook, move the yarn toward you as under the Tunisian hook so it is positioned behind the Tunisian hook *(Fig. 12b)*, hook yarn and pull through loop on hook (**ch 1 made**).

Fig. 12b

The first cast on stitch is made *(Fig. 12c)*.

Fig. 12c

Repeat this process *(Figs. 12a-c)* until you have completed all except the last cast on stitch required.

Place the loop from the standard hook onto the Tunisian hook *(Fig. 12d)*.

Fig. 12d

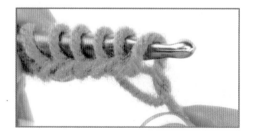

CHANGING COLORS

To change colors on the return pass, close across to last 2 stitches. Drop the old yarn and with the new yarn *(Fig. 13)*, yarn over and draw through 2 loops on hook.

Fig. 13

SLIP STITCH BIND OFF

Insert hook as for tss under next vertical bar, YO and pull loop through both loops on hook *(Fig. 14)*.

Fig. 14

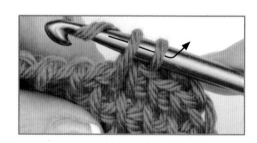

CROCHET STITCHES
SLIP STITCH *(abbreviated slip st)*

Insert hook in stitch indicated, YO and draw through stitch and through loop on hook *(Fig. 15)*.

Fig. 15

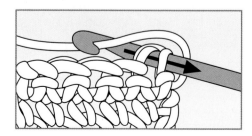

SINGLE CROCHET (abbreviated sc)

Insert hook in stitch indicated, YO and pull up a loop, YO and draw through both loops on hook (Fig. 16).

Fig. 16

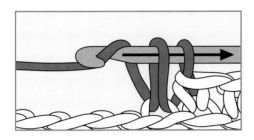

DOUBLE CROCHET (abbreviated dc)

YO, insert hook in stitch indicated, YO and pull up a loop (3 loops on hook), YO and draw through 2 loops on hook (Fig. 17a), YO and draw through remaining 2 loops on hook (Fig. 17b).

Fig. 17a

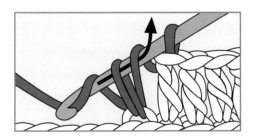

Fig. 17b

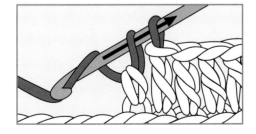

JOINING WITH SC

When instructed to join with sc, begin with a slip knot on hook. Insert hook in stitch indicated, YO and pull up a loop, YO and draw through both loops on hook (Figs. 18a & b).

Fig. 18a

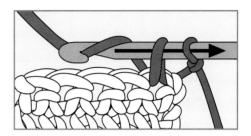

Fig. 18b

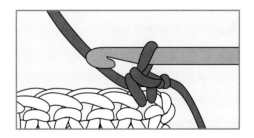

BLOCKING

Check the yarn label for any special instructions about blocking. Place your shawl on a clean terry towel over a flat surface and shape it to size. Place a damp cloth on top and hold a hand held steamer or a steam iron just above the item and steam it thoroughly. Never let the weight of the iron touch the shawl because it will flatten the stitches. Allow the shawl to dry flat, away from the heat or sun.

YARN INFORMATION

The Shawls in this book were made using various weights of yarn. Any brand of the weight specified may be used. It is best to refer to the yardage/meters when determining how many balls or skeins to purchase. Remember, to arrive at the finished size, it is the GAUGE/TENSION that is important, not the brand of yarn.

For your convenience, listed below are the specific yarns used to create our photography models.

EXPANDING VEES
Red Heart® Luster Sheen™
Black - #0002 Black
Cream - #0007 Vanilla

CABLES & HEART
LB Collection® Superwash Merino
#174 Spring Leaf

AUTUMN EMBRACE
Patons® ColorWul™
#90521 Countryside

HOT PINK LACE
LB Collection® Cotton Bamboo
#139 Hibiscus

SILVER SHIMMER
Patons® Metallic™
#95044 Pewter

POPOVER WEDGES
Red Heart® Boutique® Treasure™
 #1901 Mosiac

RED HOT WRAP
Red Heart® Anne Geddes Baby™
#0902 Ladybug

FAIR ISLE WINTER CAPELET
Lion Brand® Martha Stewart Crafts™/MC
Extra Soft Wool Blend
Cream - #599 Buttermilk
Dk Blue - #510 Sailor Blue
Blue - #507 Winter Sky
Grey - #550 Gray Pearl

We have made every effort to ensure that these instructions are accurate and complete. We cannot, however, be responsible for human error, typographical mistakes, or variations in individual work.